Workbook

Intended to accompany the book:

Success Skills for Teen Girls

The Teen Girl Survival Guide Book to Motivation and Self-Confidence

By

Lisa Wise  Love your Life

Chapter 1: Getting to Know YOU

"Always be a first-rate version of yourself, instead of a second-rate version of somebody else." - Judy Garland

Reflections on Questions:

_____

_____

_____

_____

Inspirational notes:

_____

_____

_____

_____

Quiz 1: Self Discovery. Your result and reflections:

_____

_____

_____

_____

_____

_____

Exercise 1: Positive Traits

1. *List down traits that resonate with you the most. It could be kindness, determination, creativity, resilience, empathy, courage, humor, intelligence, honesty, patience, optimism or others.*

_____

_____

2. *Choose three traits that feel the most genuine to you.*

_____

3. *For each trait, think of a time when it was on full display. Maybe it was when helping a friend in need or when finishing a challenging project. These moments serve as reminders of the strength within.*

_____

_____

_____

Reflections:

_____

_____

_____

Inspirational notes:

_____

_____

_____

Self Love Affirmations:

_____

_____

_____

Exercise 2: Values

1. *List down qualities and beliefs that feel important. It could be honesty, creativity, kindness, courage or others.*

_____

_____

2. *Reflect on each one. Does thinking about it bring a smile? Does it resonate with past decisions or actions?*

_____

3. *Choose your top two values. The ones that feel like a true reflection of who you are.*

_____

Reflections:

_____

_____

_____

Inspirational notes:

_____

_____

_____

Exercise 3: Goal Setting

1. *Reflect on the top two values chosen.*

---

2. *Think of actions or achievements that align with these values.*

---

3. *Set two or three specific, realistic, and achievable goals. Remember, it's not about how big or grand the goal is; it's about how meaningful it feels.*

Reflections:

Inspirational notes:

Key Chapter Takeaway:

_____

_____

Message from my Future Self:

_____

_____

_____

_____

My Action Plan (this week)

_____

_____

_____

My Action Plan (this year)

_____

_____

_____

_____

_____

_____

Chapter 2: Be Yourself. Confidence is up for grabs

"Believe in yourself and all that you are. Know that there is something inside you that is greater than any obstacle." — *Christian D. Larson*

Reflections. Confidence or not?

_____

_____

_____

_____

Inspirational notes:

_____

_____

_____

Reflections on questions: Challenges

_____

_____

_____

_____

_____

Inspirational notes. Be True to Yourself:

_____

_____

_____

_____

_____

_____

Quiz 2: Being True to You. Your result and reflections:

_____

_____

_____

_____

_____

Exercise 4: Your Stress Reducers:

1. Choose Your Tools: *Gather a set of Post-it notes or a small notepad that you can keep close by. This will be where you'll remind yourself of the stress-reducing strategies that resonate with you.*

_____

_____

2. Select Your Strategies: *From the list, pick out three stress-reducing tips that feel most applicable to your life. Consider the situations where you feel most stressed and what could bring you the most relief.*

---

3. Write and Display: *On your Post-it notes or in your notepad, write down the three strategies you've chosen. Then, place them in areas where you'll see them regularly — like on your desk, mirror, or inside your locker. Let these visible reminders serve as your daily stress-reducing prompts.*

4. Weekly Focus: *Each week, concentrate on one of the strategies you've written down. Practice it consistently throughout the week and observe any changes in how you feel and how you handle stress.*

---

5. Celebrate and Reflect: *At the end of each week, take a moment to celebrate your efforts and reflect on how the strategy has impacted your stress levels. Make a note of any changes and consider if you'd like to carry on with this strategy or try a new one the following week.*

Inspirational notes:

Practical Tips. Becoming the Best You:

_____

_____

_____

_____

_____

_____

_____

_____

Quiz Time! What's your go-to emotion?

_____

_____

Inspirational notes:

_____

_____

_____

_____

_____

_____

Exercise 5: Emotional, Mental and Physical Strengthening

From the insights of "Becoming the best emotional/physical/mental you," jot down two tips that resonate with you most. These should be tips that you believe will help to strengthen you in these 3 areas.

_____

_____

_____

_____

_____

Reflections. Steps to apply your tips in daily life:

_____

_____

_____

_____

Inspirational notes:

_____

_____

_____

_____

_____

Key Chapter Takeaway:

_____

Message from my Future Self:

_____

_____

_____

My Action Plan (this week)

_____

_____

_____

My Action Plan (this year)

_____

_____

_____

_____

_____

Chapter 3: Acts of Kindness come back to you

"In a world where you can be anything, be kind." - Unknown

Reflections. Kind or not?

_____

_____

_____

_____

Inspirational notes:

_____

_____

_____

_____

Key takeaways:

_____

_____

_____

_____

_____

_____

Inspirational notes. Daring to be Different:

_____

_____

_____

_____

_____

_____

_____

_____

Exercise 6: The Kindness Challenge:

One Act a Day: _Every day, do one kind thing for someone else. It doesn't have to be big. Remember, even small gestures can have a big impact._

Week 1 Date	Kindness act & reaction	Reflection: How did this make you feel?

Exercise 6: *The Kindness Challenge continued:*

Week 2 Date	Kindness act & reaction	Reflection: How did this make you feel?

Week 3 Date	Kindness act & reaction	Reflection: How did this make you feel?

Exercise 6. *The Kindness Challenge continued:*

Week 4 Date	Kindness act & reaction	Reflection: How did this make you feel?

Reflections. How did this change your daily life?

_____

_____

_____

_____

_____

_____

_____

Inspirational notes. Diversity and Inclusion:

_____
_____
_____
_____
_____
_____
_____
_____
_____
_____

Exercise 7: Inclusive Language

1. Spot the Difference: *Read a paragraph from your favorite book. Can you find words or phrases that might make someone feel left out? How can you change them to be more inclusive?*

_____
_____

2. Switch Roles: *Imagine being from a different country or having a different religion. Write a short story from that perspective. How would you want people to talk to or about you?*

_____
_____
_____
_____

Exercise 7. *Continued:*

_____

_____

_____

_____

_____

_____

_____

Reflections. Steps to apply your tips in daily life:

_____

_____

Inspirational notes:

_____

_____

_____

_____

_____

_____

Key Chapter Takeaway:

_____

_____

Message from my Future Self:

_____

_____

_____

_____

My Action Plan (this week)

_____

_____

_____

_____

My Action Plan (this year)

_____

_____

_____

_____

_____

_____

Chapter 4: Good Communication is Key

"Too often we underestimate the power of touch, a smile, a kind word, a listening ear… all of which have the potential to turn a life around." - Leo Buscaglia

Reflections:

_____

_____

_____

_____

Inspirational notes:

_____

_____

_____

_____

Exercise 8: Good Conversation

_____

_____

_____

_____

_____

Tips for Self Expression:

_____
_____
_____
_____
_____
_____
_____
_____

Reflections. Understanding Compromise:

_____
_____
_____
_____
_____

Inspirational notes:

_____
_____
_____
_____

Inspirational notes. Checking In:

_____

_____

_____

Exercise 9: Art of Checking In

*1. Select two people for your check-in. 2. Reach out to them with a message or a call.
3. Ask how they are doing and genuinely listen to their response.*

Date	Who	How did this make you feel? How were they impacted?

Reflections:

_____

_____

Inspirational notes:

_____

_____

_____

Key Chapter Takeaway:

_____

_____

Message from my Future Self:

_____

_____

_____

_____

My Action Plan (this week)

_____

_____

_____

My Action Plan (this year)

_____

_____

_____

_____

_____

Chapter 5: Finding and Keeping that Special Friend

"Friendship is born at that moment when one person says to another, 'What! You too? I thought I was the only one.'" - C.S. Lewis

Reflections to Questions:

_____
_____
_____
_____

Inspirational notes:

_____
_____
_____
_____

Quiz 3: How to Recognize a Good Friend. Your results and reflections:

_____
_____
_____
_____
_____
_____

My Insights on friendship:

_____

_____

_____

_____

_____

_____

_____

Tips for Overcoming Fear of Rejection:

_____

_____

_____

_____

Inspirational notes:

_____

_____

_____

_____

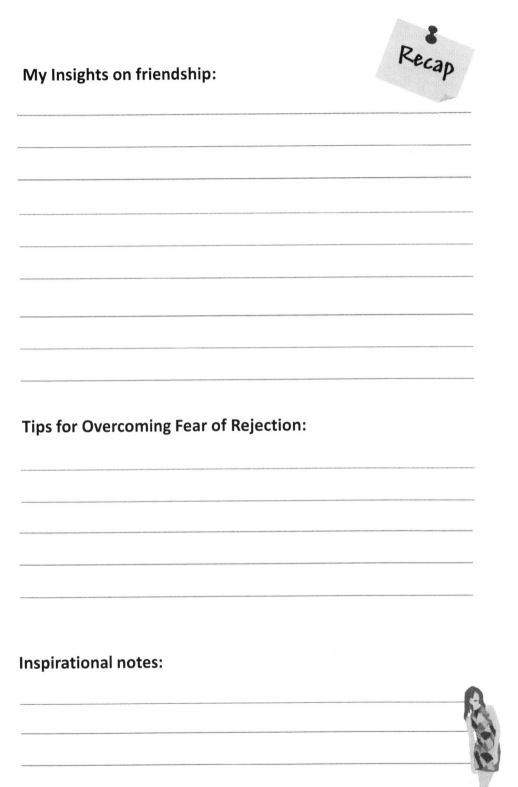

Quiz 4: How to be a Good Friend. My results and reflections:

_____

_____

_____

_____

_____

_____

_____

Inspirational notes:

_____

_____

_____

_____

_____

_____

_____

_____

Key Chapter Takeaway:

_____

_____

Message from my Future Self:

_____

_____

_____

_____

My Action Plan (this week)

_____

_____

_____

_____

My Action Plan (this year)

_____

_____

_____

_____

_____

_____

Chapter 6: Friend Groups. Tips and Tricks

"In the sweetness of friendship let there be laughter and sharing of pleasures. For in the dew of little things the heart finds its morning and is refreshed." — Khalil Gibran

Reflections:

_____

_____

_____

_____

Inspirational notes:

_____

_____

_____

_____

Exercise 10: Compromise in a Group. Inspirational notes:

_____

_____

_____

_____

_____

Exercise 11: Navigating Cliques. Inspirational notes:

_____

_____

_____

_____

_____

_____

Tips for Navigating cliques:

_____

_____

_____

_____

Quiz 5: Handling Peer Pressure. Your answers and reflections:

_____

_____

_____

_____

_____

_____

_____

My Peer Pressure Action Plan:

_____

_____

_____

_____

Message from my Future Self:

_____

_____

_____

_____

Key Chapter Takeaway:

_____

_____

My Action Plan (this year)

_____

_____

_____

_____

_____

_____

Chapter 7: When It Gets Icky

"No person is your friend who demands your silence, or denies your right to grow."
— Alice Walker

Reflections to Questions:

Tips – Handling Mean Girls:

Exercise 12: Spotting Toxic People

Tick which behaviours you think could be toxic in a friendship:
1. Gossiping about others constantly.
2. Offering support only when it's convenient for them.
3. Regularly cancelling plans at the last minute.
4. Always insisting on having their way in group decisions.
5. Listening attentively and giving advice when you're facing challenges.
6. Sharing your personal information with others without consent.
7. Encouraging you to try new things and step out of your comfort zone.
8. Making hurtful jokes at your expense, even after you've asked them to stop.

Reflection on toxic friends and steps to take:

_____

_____

_____

_____

_____

_____

Action Plan:

_____

_____

_____

Tips for Recognizing a Frenemy:

_____

_____

_____

_____

_____

Inspirational notes:

_____

_____

_____

_____

Key Chapter Takeaway:

_____

_____

Message from my Future Self:

_____

_____

_____

_____

My Action Plan (this week)

_____

_____

_____

_____

My Action Plan (this year)

_____

_____

_____

_____

_____

Chapter 8: Use Social Media Wisely

"Don't use social media to impress people; use it to impact people." - Dave Willis

Reflections:

_____

_____

_____

_____

Tips – Avoiding Cyberbullying:

_____

_____

_____

Quiz 6: Are You Addicted to Social Media? Your answers and reflections:

_____

_____

_____

_____

_____

_____

_____

Tips on Best Habits for Social Media Use:

_____

_____

_____

_____

_____

Action Plan to Balance Social Media with Real Life:

_____

_____

Inspirational notes – Making Friends on Social Media:

_____

_____

_____

_____

_____

Reflections:

_____

_____

_____

_____

Key Chapter Takeaway:

_____

Message from my Future Self:

_____

_____

_____

_____

My Action Plan (this week)

_____

_____

_____

_____

My Action Plan (this year)

_____

_____

_____

_____

_____

_____

Chapter 9: Transition to Independence

"Seek wisdom like hidden treasure"

Reflections:

_____

_____

_____

Inspirational notes – What would my Parents Know?

_____

_____

_____

_____

_____

Reflections – Balancing Independence and Guidance:

_____

_____

_____

_____

Inspirational notes – What is a Mentor?

_____

_____

_____

_____

_____

Tips – Independent or Guided Decision Making?

_____

_____

_____

_____

_____

_____

Reflections:

_____

_____

_____

_____

_____

Key Chapter Takeaway:

_____

_____

Message from my Future Self:

_____

_____

_____

_____

My Action Plan (this week)

_____

_____

_____

_____

My Action Plan (this year)

_____

_____

_____

_____

_____

_____

Chapter 10: Being the Fabulous You

"Embrace your uniqueness and let your light shine."

Reflections:

_____

_____

_____

_____

Inspirational notes:

_____

_____

_____

_____

**Quiz 7: Readiness for Growth and Goal Achievement.
Your results and reflections:**

_____

_____

_____

_____

_____

_____

Exercise 13. Checklist to Becoming the Best You:

1.   Read through the checklist below and mark with 2 stars the points that you consider the most important.

2.   Then mark with an arrow the points that you consider need further work.

1. Self-Discovery: Celebrate Your Uniqueness

- **Understand Your Strengths and Weaknesses:** (See Chapter 1: Quiz 1, Self discovery; Exercise 1, Positive traits)

- **Explore Your Interests**: (See Chapter 1: Exercise 2, Values)

- **Acknowledge Your Feelings and Emotions:** Be aware of how you feel and why. It's okay to have a range of emotions. (See Chapter 1, Exercise 3)

2. Set Goals: Chart Your Path

- **Identify What You Want to Achieve:** (See Chapter 1: Exercise 3, Goal setting)

- **Create Actionable Steps**

- **Track Your Progress:** Keep a journal or a planner to monitor how you are advancing towards your goals.

Recap

3. Be Yourself: Authenticity is Key

- **Embrace Your Individuality:** (See Chapter 2: Quiz 2, Being true to you; Exercise 4, Stress reducers; Exercise 5, Emotional, physical and mental strengthening

- **Express Yourself:** (See Chapter 4: Exercise 8, Good conversation; Exercise 9, Check-in with people)

- **Stand Up for Your Beliefs**

4. Be Kind and Build Healthy Relationships: Connect with Others

- **Choose Friends Wisely:** (See Chapter 5: Quiz 3, Finding a good friend; Chapter 4: Exercise 9, Check-in with people; Chapter 5: Quiz 4, How to be a good friend; Chapter 6: Exercise 11, Navigating cliques; Chapter 7: Exercise 12, Spotting toxic people.)

- **Communicate Openly**

- **Be a Good Listener:** Show empathy and understanding towards others. (See Chapter 3: Exercise 6, Kindness; Exercise 7, Inclusive of other; Chapter 4: Exercise 8, Good conversation)

5. Manage Challenges: Develop Resilience

- **Face Difficulties Head-On:** (See Chapter 6: Quiz 5, Handling peer pressure.)

Exercise 13. Checklist continued:

- **Learn from Failures**

- **Seek Support when Needed**

6. Balance Independence and Guidance: Find Your Path

- **Make Decisions for Yourself**

- **Value Advice from Parents and Mentors**

- **Find a Mentor**: (See Chapter 9, examples of mentors)

7. Embrace Personal Growth: Always Evolve

- **Stay Curious and Keep Learning**

- **Reflect Regularly**

- **Celebrate Your Achievements**

8. Use Social Media Wisely: Digital Well-being

- **Be Mindful of Your Online Presence**: Post content that reflects your true self. (See Chapter 8: Quiz 6, Are you addicted to social media?)

- **Limit Screen Time**: Balance your online activities with real-world experiences. (See Chapter 8: Best habits check-list).

Exercise 13. Checklist continued:

- **Practice Safe Online Interactions**: Be cautious when sharing personal information.

9. Seek Independence and Wisdom: Grow with Guidance

- **Ask Questions and Seek Advice**: Don't hesitate to reach out for insights from experienced individuals.

- **Balance Freedom with Responsibility**: As you gain independence, be mindful of your responsibilities

10. Be Fabulous: Shine in Your Own Way

- **Follow Your Heart**: Do what makes you happy and fulfilled.

- **Spread Kindness and Positivity**: Be a source of joy and support for others.

- **Enjoy the Journey**: Remember that life is a journey, not a destination.

Reflections:

Inspirational notes. Charting your path forwards:

_____

_____

_____

_____

_____

_____

_____

_____

Reflections:

_____

_____

_____

_____

_____

_____

_____

_____

_____

Key Chapter Takeaway:

Message from my Future Self:

My Action Plan (this week)

My Action Plan (this year)

Please leave a review

Please review review "Success Skills for Teen Girls"!

This would help spread the life changing tools and tips for teen girls in this book. If you found this book useful to enhance self-understanding and launch your journey to self-confidence, friendship, and fun, then scan the QR code and leave a review.

QR code to Amazon review page

Lisa would love to hear from you!! Reach out through her Instagram: @lisawise__lovelife

Lisa's goal for every teen is happiness and to LOVE-your-LIFE!

Made in the USA
Columbia, SC
08 December 2024

48708542R00026